Contents

Introduction

Why numeracy?

Developing a strong foundation in understanding numbers is essential for all children to move forward in their education and in their awareness of the world around them. As children become familiar with how numbers work, they are able to take a more active part in our world.

Numbers can be fun for children! Simple, enjoyable numeracy activities enable them to count competently and confidently; recognize shapes, patterns, and sequences; identify and form numerals; and equate them with the appropriate quantities.

Why in English?

Learning and playing with numbers in English, and developing numerical ability through English, is a good example of holistic learning. Having children work simultaneously through English and with numbers increases their understanding in both areas, establishing a strong foundation for their future learning. Exploring numerical and mathematical concepts within an English-speaking environment will also enhance children's experience of numeracy training in their own language, transferring skills and empowering children to become agents in their own learning.

How to use the Numeracy Books

The Numeracy Books will add enrichment to the experience of early mathematics for all young learners. They can be used as a valuable numeracy supplement to any preschool English course, allowing you to work through the book at your own pace. In the books, you will find presentation, familiarization, and practice pages, consolidating and extending the children's understanding of number work.

Numeracy Book 1 provides four pages of pre-numeracy skills followed by presentation and practice of numbers 1–10, as well as review of 1–5 and 1–10. When new numbers are presented, there are opportunities for practicing formation of the numeral as well as recognizing the related quantity. Further activities practice identifying and distinguishing the numerals and equating them to the appropriate quantities by matching, counting, circling, coloring, and drawing. Listening activities give aural cues for children to identify numbers and provide the opportunity to use movement and rhythm to strengthen familiarity with number sequence. In the final two activity pages (*I can …*), children are encouraged to summarize what they have learned and feel proud of their achievements.

Activity types

Trace. / Match. / Connect.

Encourage children to trace along the dashed lines from left to right, where appropriate, following the arrows. If they find it tricky to trace with a pencil, they can follow the lines with a fingertip instead.

When they have to match or connect numerals to pictures, encourage them to stop and count first.

Find. / Circle.

Children can use their observation skills to count objects or find representations of numerals within a picture. At this stage of their development, children can demonstrate their understanding of a mathematical concept by circling the correct image or numeral from a group of options. This acts as a precursor to completing activities by writing numerals at Level 2.

Color. / Draw.

Young children will have varying levels of fine motor skills. Some will be able to color pictures very carefully, and some will color "over" a picture rather than color between the lines. Similarly, the children's ability to draw pictures freehand will be very varied. This doesn't need to be a cause for concern; it is more important that the children are engaging with and learning from the activity than coloring or drawing perfectly.

Listen.

For activities that require the children to listen for information, make sure they understand what they have to do before they listen. Demonstrate what they have to do and where. Then play the audio as many times as necessary.

Listen and clap. Listen again and draw.

The first time you play the audio, allow children simply to listen. Then play it a second time and encourage the children to clap along.

Play it again. Indicate the empty box as the children hear the final number or word. Demonstrate drawing in the box.

Repeat the procedure for the remaining lines. You may wish to encourage the children to predict what will go in the box at the end of the third line before they hear the audio for that line. They can then listen and check if their prediction was right.

Play the track again. Everyone claps and joins in.

Listen and do the actions.

Before playing the audio, make sure the children are ready to do the actions pictured on the page. Practice the actions and then try with the audio. Once the children become more confident, encourage them to join in with the words.

Number activities and games

Numeral recognition and formation

Practice numeral formation away from the page, employing gross as well as fine motor skills; for example:

- Draw numbers on each other's backs.
- Draw numbers on the ground in chalk.
- Draw numbers in sand.
- Draw numbers in the air using large arm movements. Alternatively, the teacher or children can do this while other children watch and say what the number is.
- Form numbers out of modeling clay.
- Hold up a number card and ask children to hold up the same number of fingers.

Counting

Vary the counting style; for example:

- Count and clap.
- Count and step or stamp.
- Count and bang a drum or tap a desk gently.
- Count silently by moving lips and showing fingers.
- Count items around the school and adjacent areas.
- The teacher or one of the children claps, taps the desk, or bangs a drum. Children listen and say how many beats they heard.

When young children are counting items or pictures, encourage them to be slow and careful, as the speed at which they count aloud is often different from the speed at which they move their hands or fingers from item to item.

Number order

Give opportunities for children to practice using numbers in the correct order; for example:

- Have children sit in a circle and say the numbers in order.
- Have children sit in a circle and roll a ball to each other, saying the next number each time the ball is rolled.
- Give number cards to different children and ask them to say their numbers in order.
- Give number cards to different children and have them arrange themselves in order.
- Place number cards around the room, either pinned to walls or placed on different tables. Ask the children to stand next to number *1* and then follow a path to visit the remaining numbers in order.

With confident classes, you can ask the children to do the activities using the numbers in reverse order.

Quantities

Practice equating numbers with quantities; for example:

- Give a number and ask children to form groups of that number.
- Give a number and ask children to hold up, find, or bring you that number of items.
- Give a number and ask children to clap, stamp, step, jump, or pat their heads that number of times.
- Give a number and ask children to take that number of items (e.g., pencils) out of a bag or pillow case without looking inside it.
- Arrange piles of items, e.g., four blocks and seven blocks. Give a number and ask children to point to or stand next to the correct pile.

How many?

Play counting games. Encourage the rest of the class to count as one child does an activity; for example:

- How many cups can the children stack?
- How many times can they bounce a balloon or throw and catch it?
- How many bubbles can they blow?
- How many items can they find; e.g., windows in a classroom, trees in a playground, or hoops in a gym.
- How many times can they hop / jump, etc.?
- Hold up fingers (or a number card) behind your back, or hold small items in your hand, so that the children can't see how many you are holding. Ask the children *How many?* The children call out their guesses (or hold up fingers to show their guesses). Show the children your fingers / items. Repeat the game, inviting children to hold up fingers or hold items for the rest of the class to guess.

1 Trace.

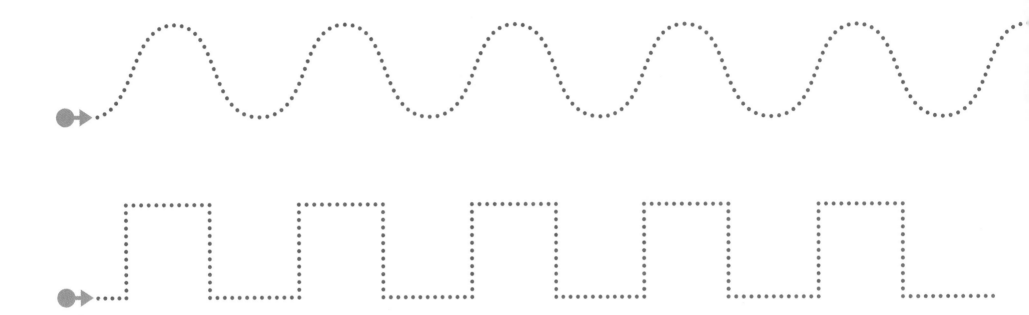

2 Draw your own pattern.

1 Look. Circle the picture that is different.

1 Trace and color the circles.

Pre-numeracy skills

1 Look. What's next? Draw.

1 Trace **number 1**.

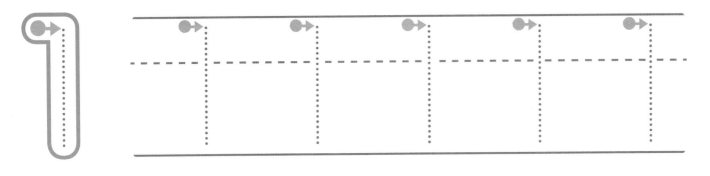

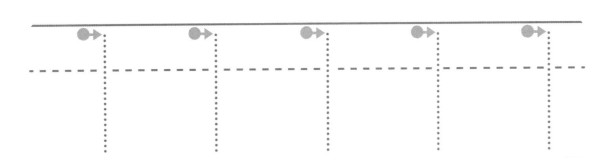

2 Color and count.

1 one

3 Circle **number 1**.

3   4      2   5

1 Trace **number 2**.

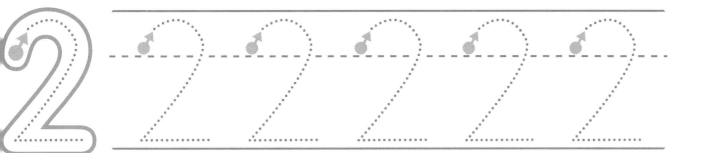

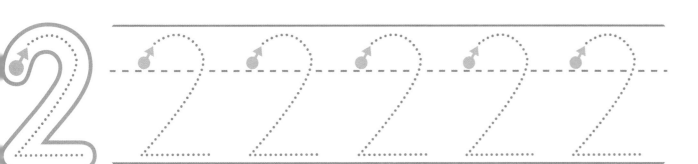

2 two

3 Circle **number 2**.

2   **5**   **3**   **1**   **4**

1 Trace the numbers. Count and match.

2 Trace and say.

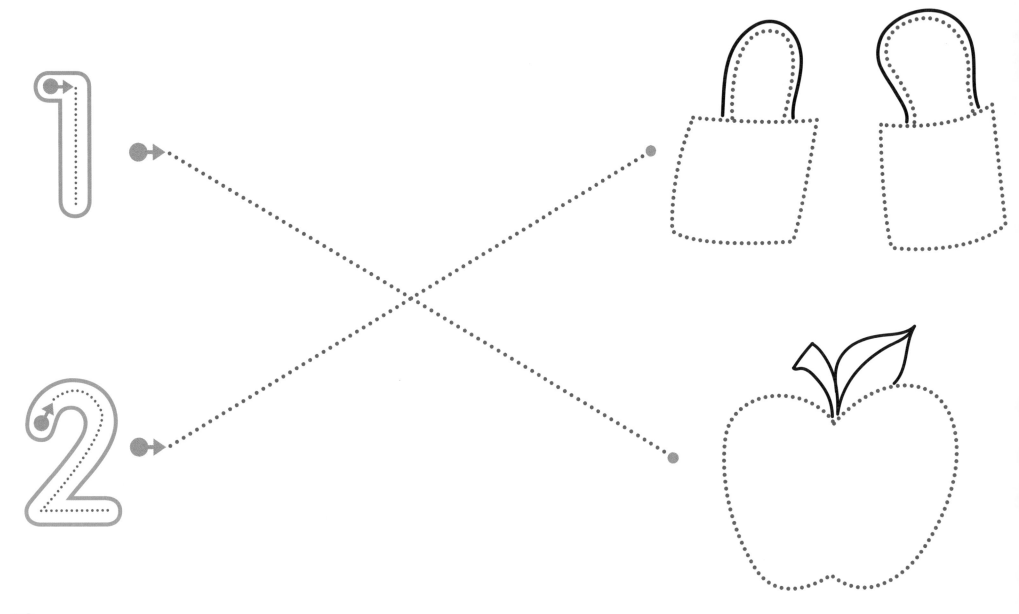

1 Trace, count, and say. Circle **1** or **2**.

1 Find the faces and count. Color **1** or **2**.

2 Complete the face for you.

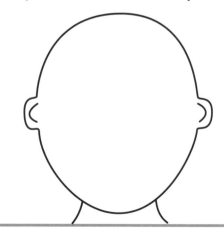

1 🔊001 Listen and clap. **2** 🔊002 Listen again and draw.

1 Trace **number 3**.

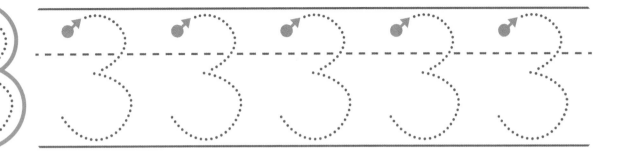

3 3 3 3 3 3

3 3 3 3 3 3

2 Color and count.

3 three

---

3 Circle **number 3**.

4   2   **3**   5   1

1 Trace **number 4**.

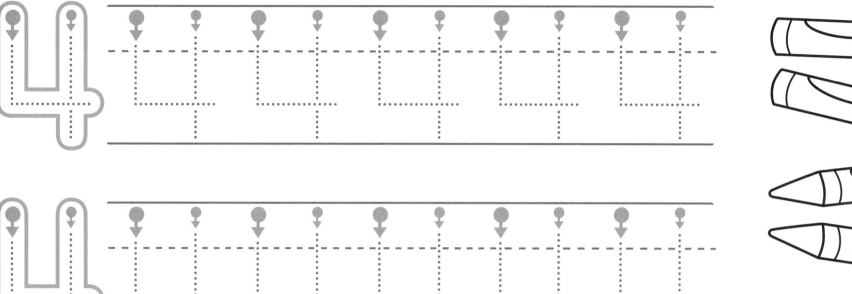

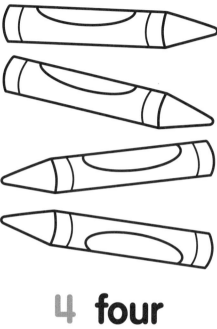

4 four

3 Circle **number 4**.

3   4   1   2   5

1 Trace the numbers. Count and match.

2 Color and say.

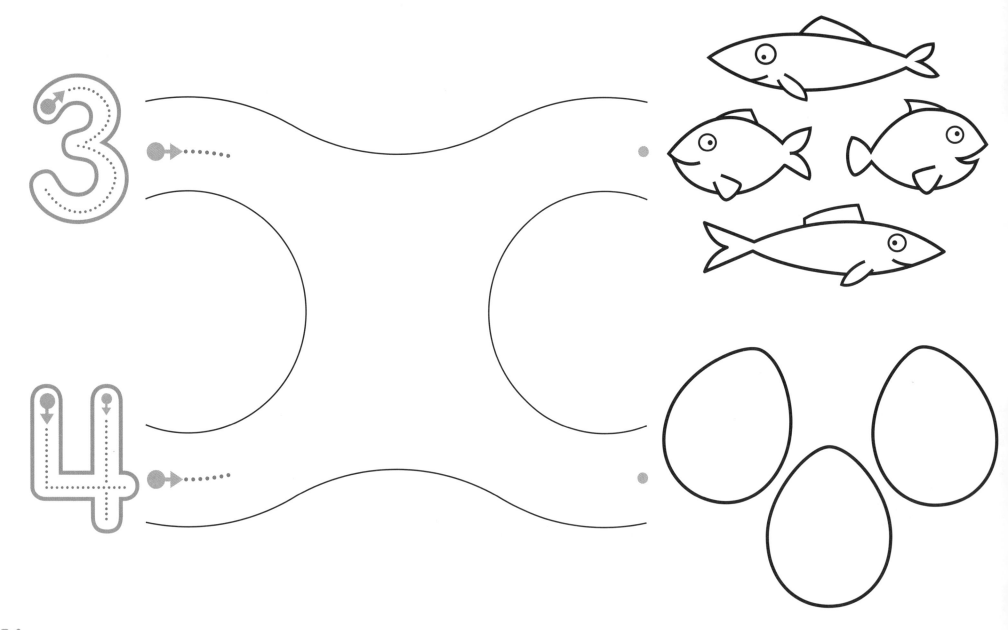

1 🔊003 Listen and circle.

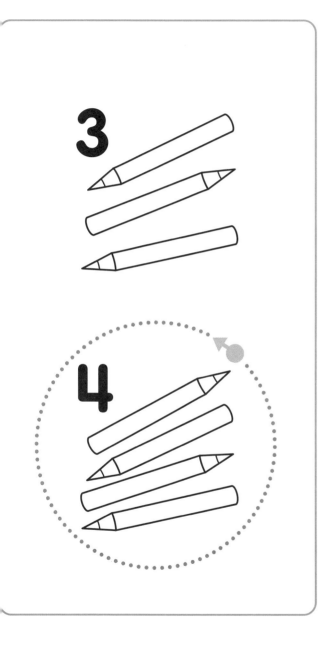

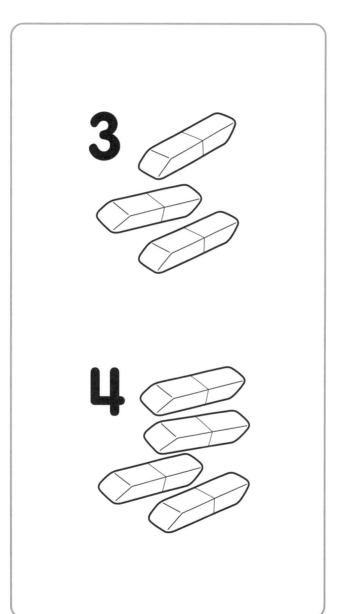

1 Find, count, and color.

2 Circle your favorite book.

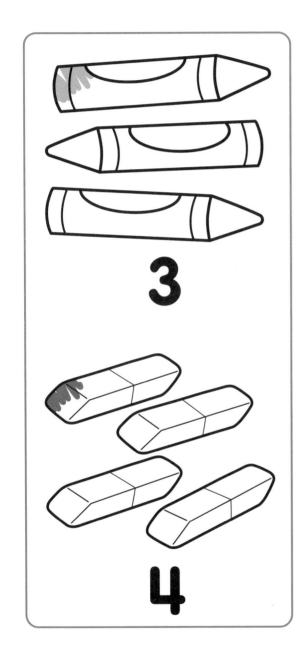

3

4

1 🔊 004 Listen and clap. **2** 🔊 005 Listen again and draw.

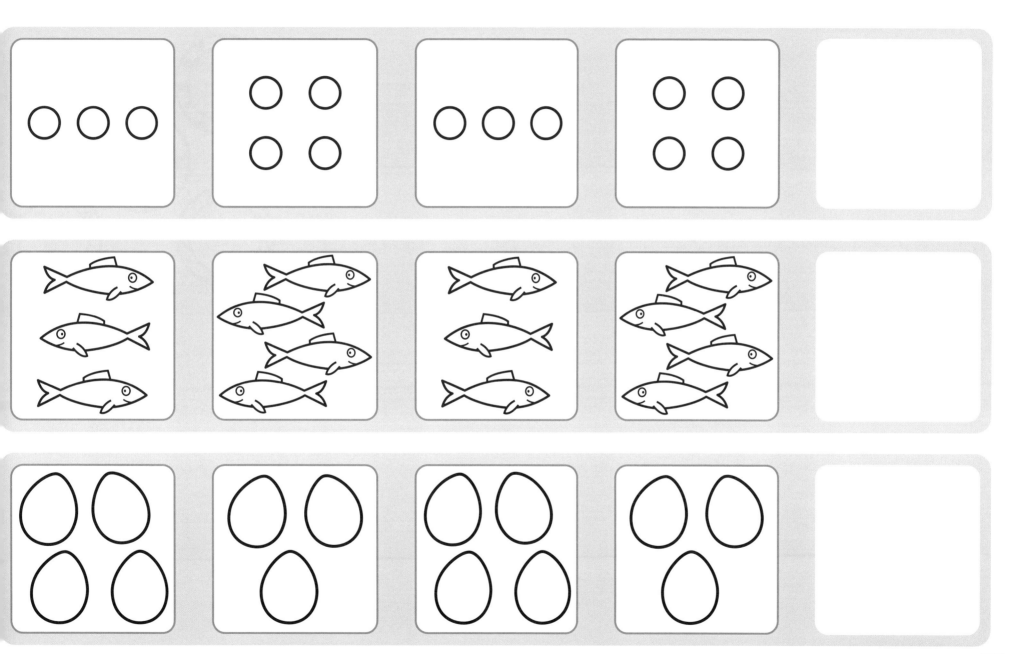

1 Trace **number 5**.

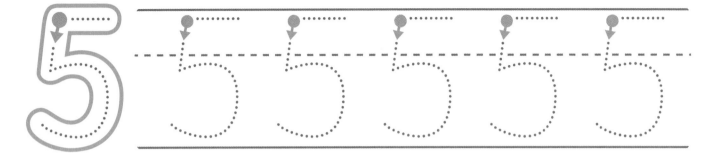

2 Color and count.

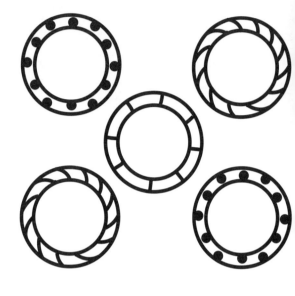

5 five

3 Circle **number 5**.

1

3

2

5

4

1 Color and connect the groups of **5**.

1 Count the people in the family. Circle the number.   **2** Color the picture.

1   2   3   4   5

1 🔊006 Trace. Listen, count, and circle.

1 Color and say the numbers. Find the numbers in the picture and color.

1 2 3 4 5

Trace, say, and match.

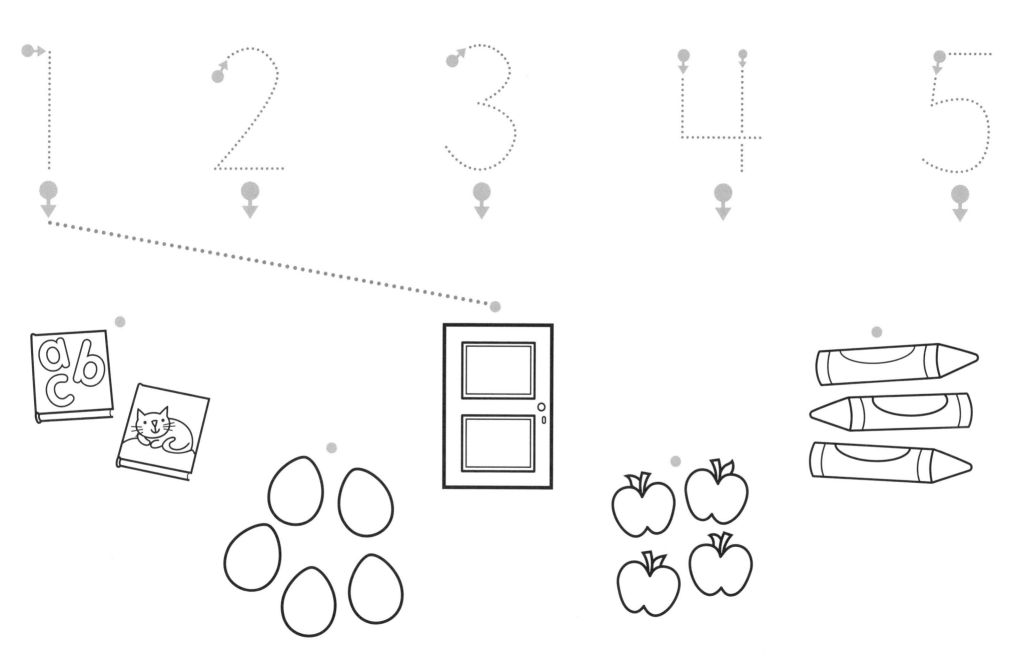

1 Count and circle the number.

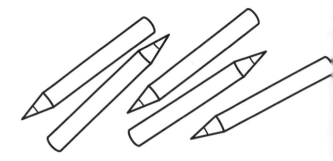

1   **2**   3   4   5

1   2   3   4   5

1   2   3   4   5

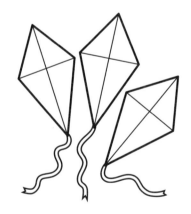

1   2   3   4   5

1   2   3   4   5

1 Look at the number and draw.

2

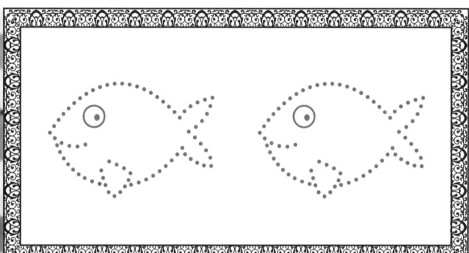

5

3

1 Connect the numbers. **2** Color the picture. Choose your favorite colors.

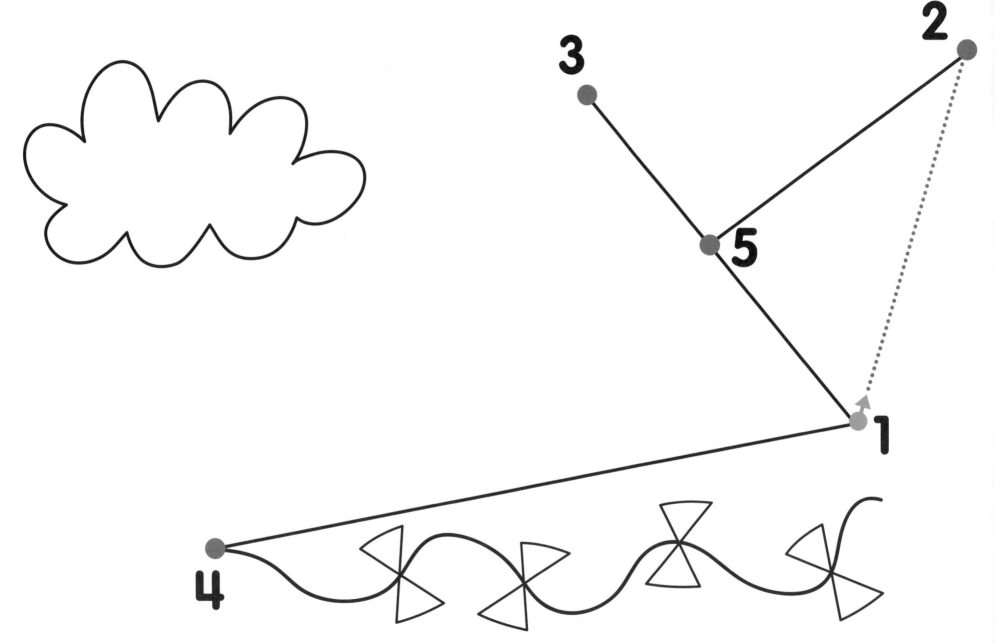

1 Trace the numbers. Connect in order.   **2** 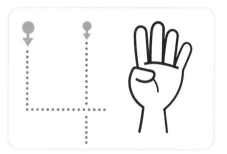007 Listen and do the actions.

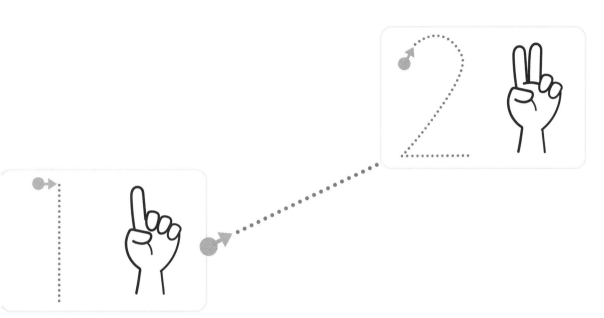

1 Trace **number 6**.

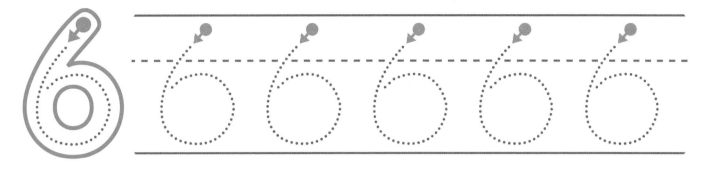

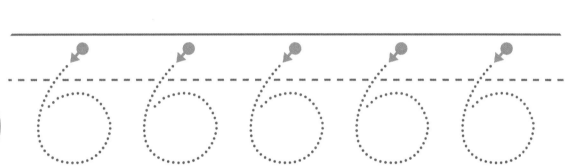

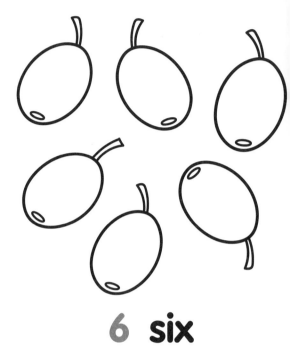

6 six

3 Circle **number 6**.

5   4   **3**   1   **6**   **2**

1 Trace **number 7**.

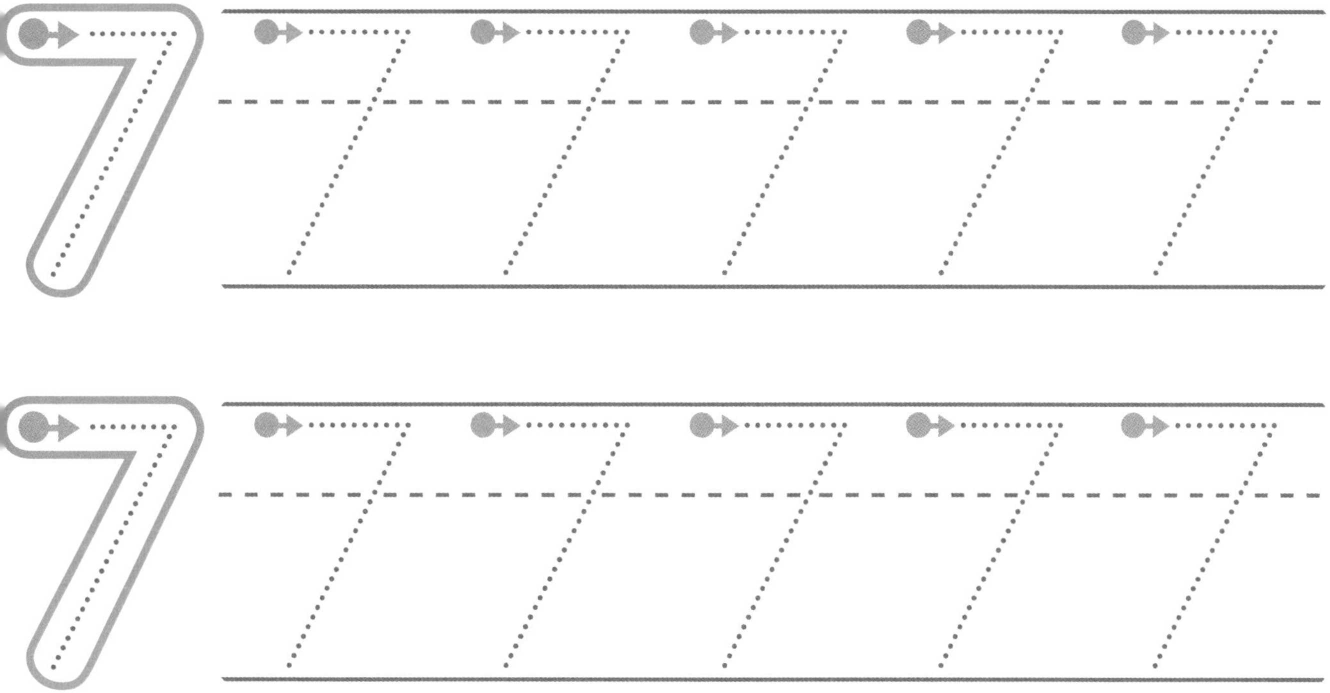

2 Color and count.

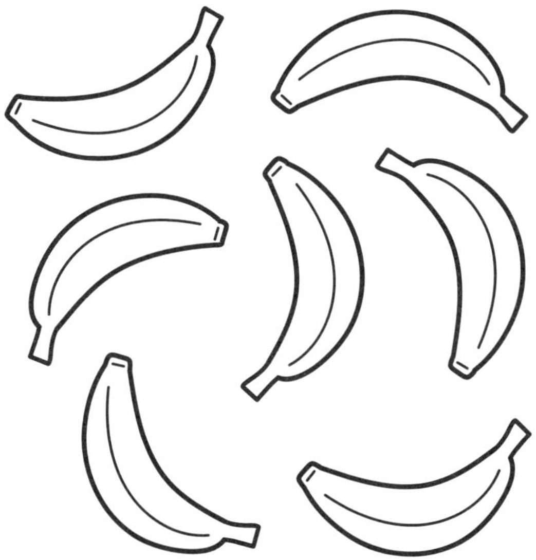

7 seven

3 Circle **number 7**.

3   4   6   1   7

2   5

1 Trace the numbers. Count and match.

2 Color and say.

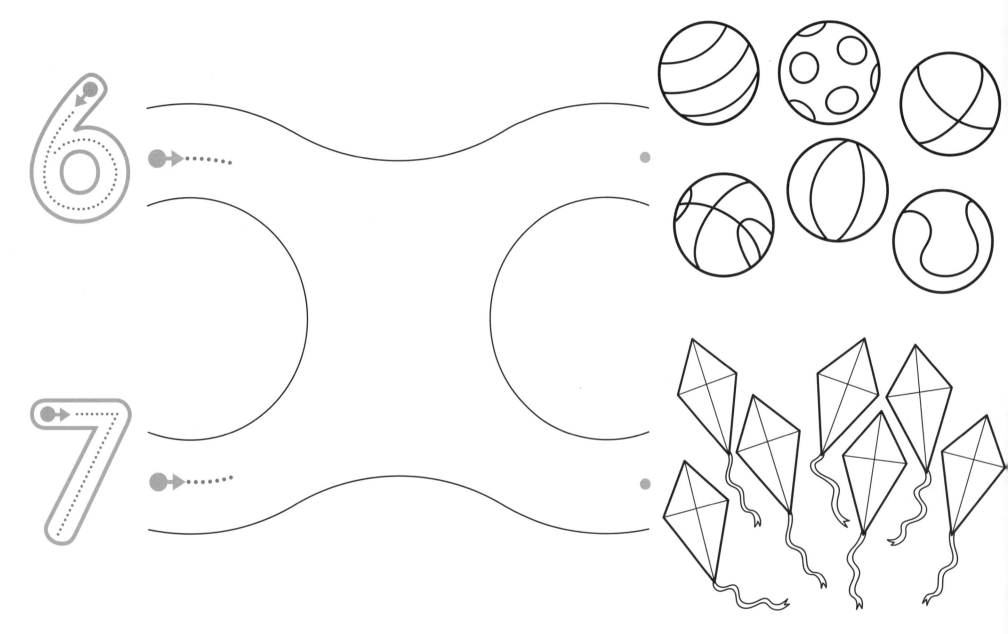

1 Look at the number and draw.   **2** Do you like mangoes ? Do you like bananas ? Draw your face.

7

6

1 Connect the books 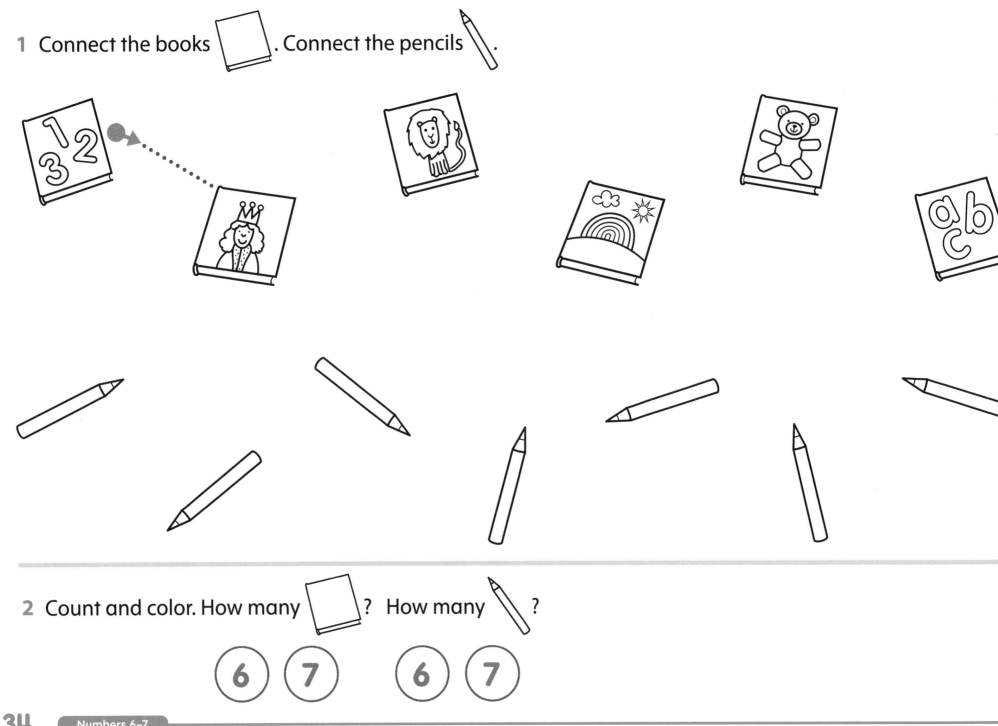. Connect the pencils.

2 Count and color. How many ☐? How many ✏?

6   7   6   7

1 🔊008 Listen and clap.   2 🔊009 Listen again and draw.

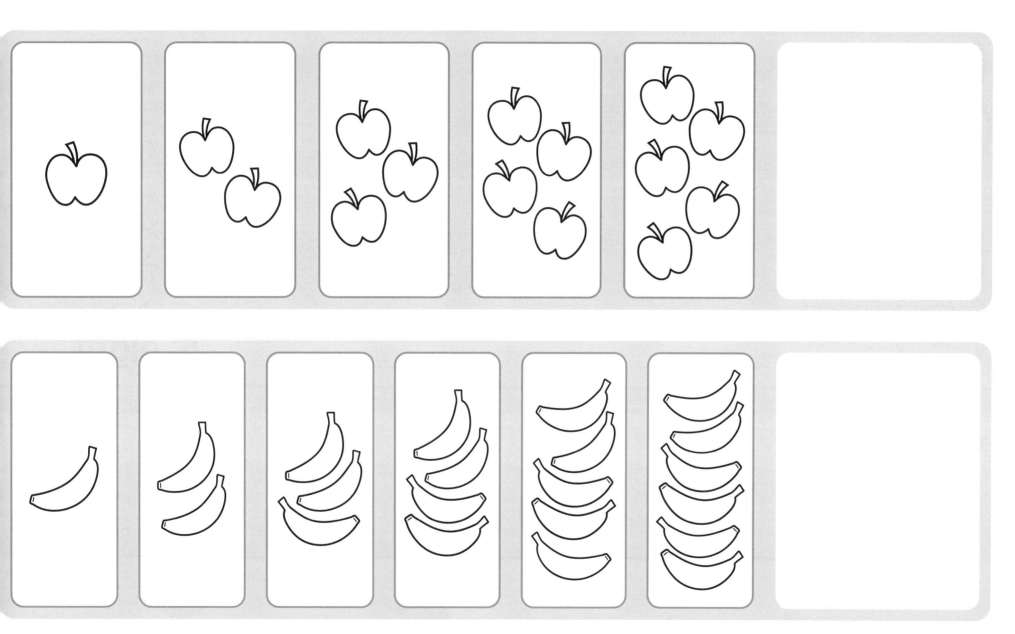

1 Trace **number 8**.

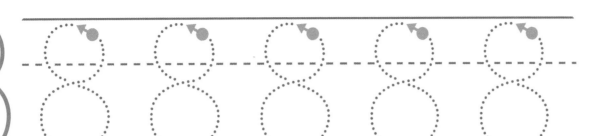

2 Color and count.

8 eight

3 Circle **number 8**.

7   4   1   6   5   2   3   8

1 Trace **number 9**.

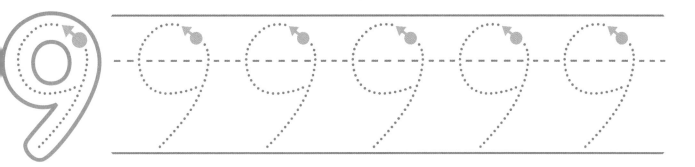

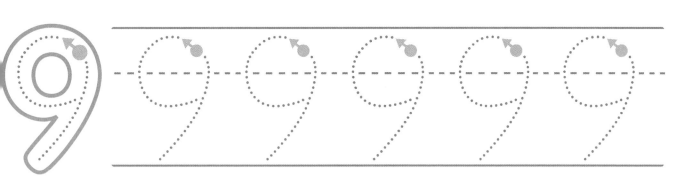

2 Color and count.

9 nine

3 Circle **number 9**.

3 6 4 9 1 8 2 7 5

1 Trace the numbers. Count and match.

2 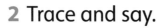 Trace and say.

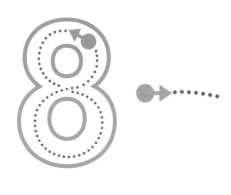

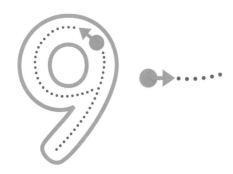

1 🔊010 Listen and circle.

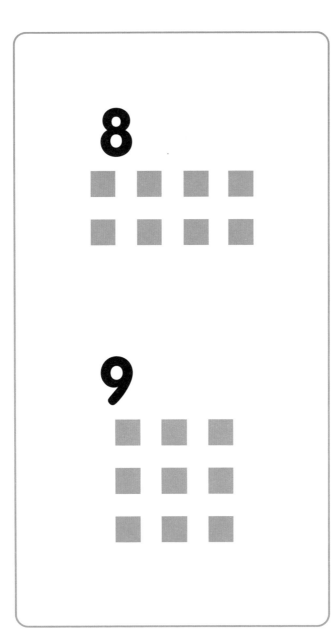

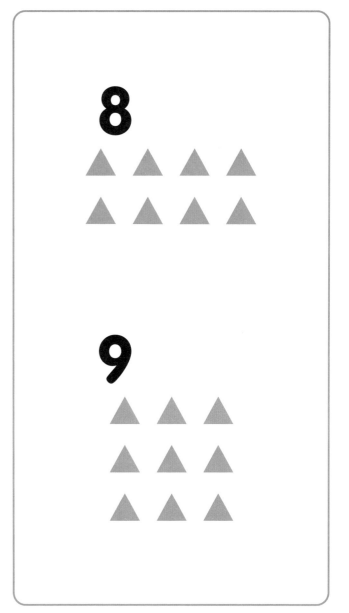

1 Find, count, and color.

2 Design your robot.

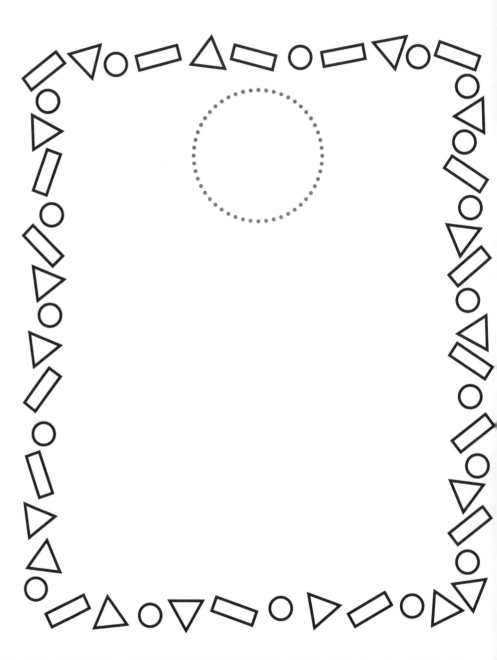

1 🔊011 Listen and draw.

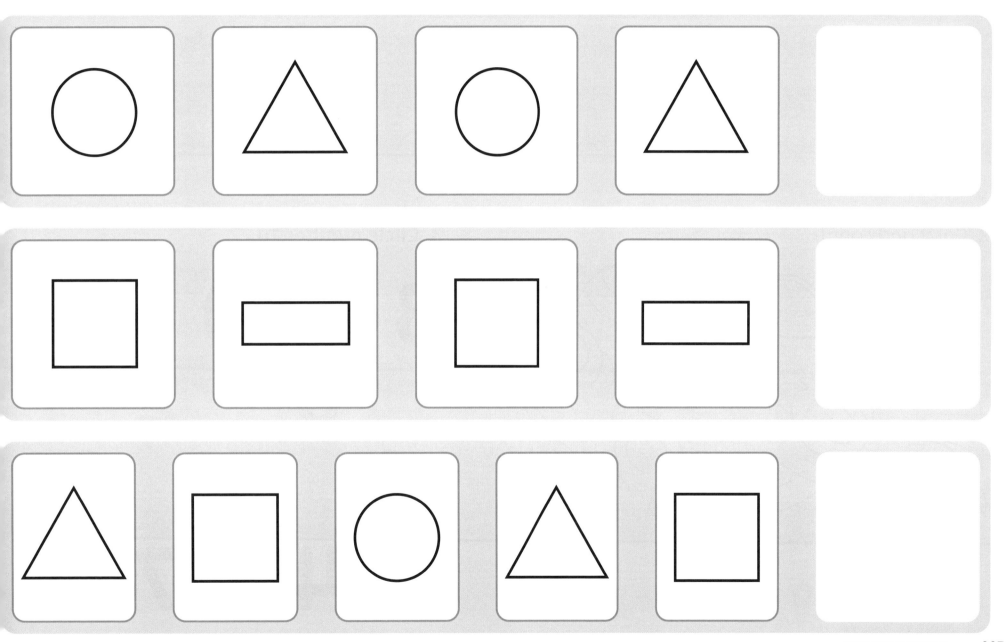

1 Trace **number 10**.

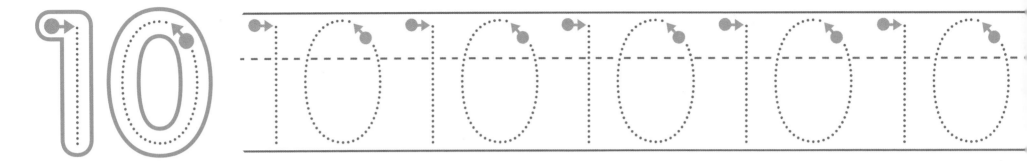

2 Color and count.

10 ten

3 Circle **number 10**.

8 10 5

6 2

3 1 9

4 7

1 Count the flowers. Circle the number. **2** Color the picture.

1 2 3 4 5 6 7 8 9 10

1 Look at the number. Count and color.

3

7

10

1 🔊**012** Trace. Listen, count, and circle.

1 Color and say the numbers. Find the numbers in the picture and color.

6 7 8 9 10

1 Trace, say, and match.

1 Connect the numbers. Color the picture.　**2** Do you like cats? Complete the face for you.

1 Look at the number and draw.

4

3

7

1 Count and circle the number.

    1   2   3   4   5   ⑥   7   8   9   10

    1   2   3   4   5   6   7   8   9   10

    1   2   3   4   5   6   7   8   9   10

    1   2   3   4   5   6   7   8   9   10

1 Trace the numbers. Connect in order.   **2** 🔊 013 Listen and do the actions.

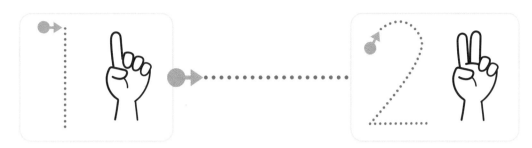

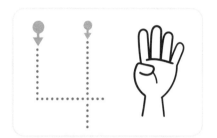

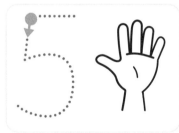

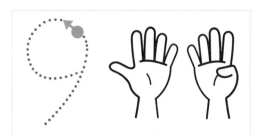

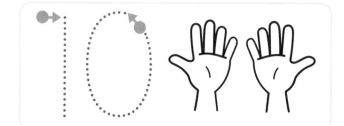

1 Trace the numbers and count.

2 Say and color the numbers.

1 2 3 4 5 6 7 8 9 10

3 Find and count.

Audio transcripts

Page 13

◄))001–002 Listen and clap. Listen again and draw.

1 (1 clap), 2 (2 claps), 1 (1 clap), 2 (2 claps), 1 (1 clap)

2 apples (2 claps), 1 apple (1 clap), 2 apples (2 claps), 1 apple (1 clap), 2 apples (2 claps)

1 bag (1 clap), 2 bags (2 claps), 1 bag (1 clap), 2 bags (2 claps), 1 bag (1 clap)

Page 17

◄))003 Listen and circle.

4 pencils

3 erasers

4 books

Page 19

◄))004–005 Listen and clap. Listen again and draw.

3 (3 claps), 4 (4 claps), 3 (3 claps), 4 (4 claps), 3 (3 claps)

3 fish (3 claps), 4 fish (4 claps), 3 fish (3 claps), 4 fish (4 claps), 3 fish (3 claps)

4 eggs (4 claps), 3 eggs (3 claps), 4 eggs (4 claps), 3 eggs (3 claps), 4 eggs (4 claps)

Page 23

◄))006 Listen, count, and circle.

5 insects

Page 29

◄))007 Listen and do the actions.

1, 2, 3, 4, 5 (2 beats per number)

1, 2, 3, 4, 5 (1 beat per number)

Page 35

◄))008–009 Listen and clap. Listen again and draw.

1 apple (1 clap), 2 apples (2 claps), 3 apples (3 claps), 4 apples (4 claps),

5 apples (5 claps), 6 apples (6 claps)

1 banana (1 clap), 2 bananas (2 claps), 3 bananas (3 claps), 4 bananas (4 claps),

5 bananas (5 claps), 6 bananas (6 claps), 7 bananas (7 claps)

Page 39

◄))010 Listen and circle.

8 circles

9 squares

9 triangles

Page 41

◄))011 Listen and draw.

A circle, a triangle, a circle, a triangle, a circle.

A square, a rectangle, a square, a rectangle, a square.

A triangle, a square, a circle, a triangle, a square, a circle.

Page 45

◄))012 Listen, count, and circle.

10 birds

Page 51

◄))013 Listen and do the actions.

1, 2, 3, 4, 5, 6, 7, 8, 9, 10 (2 beats per number)

1, 2, 3, 4, 5, 6, 7, 8, 9, 10 (1 beat per number)

Answer key

Page 5
1st row – 3rd picture
2nd row – 4th picture
3rd row – 2nd picture

Page 7
1st row – triangle
2nd row – straight line
3rd row – circle

Page 10
1 – apple; 2 – bags

Page 11
2 eyes, 2 ears, 1 nose, 1 mouth

Page 12
2 sad, 1 tired, 1 angry, 2 happy

Page 13
1st row – 1 dot
2nd row – 2 apples
3rd row – 1 bag

Page 16
3 – eggs; 4 – fish

Page 17
4 pencils
3 erasers
4 books

Page 18
Children color 3 crayons blue in the picture.
Children color 4 erasers gray in the picture.

Page 19
1st row – 3 dots
2nd row – 3 fish
3rd row – 4 eggs

Page 22
5

Page 23
5 insects

Page 24
Children choose a different color for each of the numbers. They find the numbers in the picture and color them, using the same colors.

Page 25
1 – door
2 – books
3 – crayons
4 – apples
5 – eggs

Page 26
2 hoops
5 pencils
1 leaf
3 kites
4 insects

Page 27
2 fish
5 apples
3 eggs

Page 32
6 – balls
7 – kites

Page 33
7 mangoes
6 bananas

Page 34
6 books
7 pencils

Page 35
6 apples
7 bananas

Page 38
8 – balls
9 – balloons

Page 39
8 circles
9 squares
9 triangles

Page 40
Children color 8 triangles blue in the picture.
Children color 9 rectangles gray in the picture.

Page 41
1st row – circle
2nd row – square
3rd row – circle

Page 43
10

Page 44
Children color 3 trees, 7 birds, and 10 umbrellas.

Page 45
10 birds

Page 46
Children choose a different color for each of the numbers. They find the numbers in the picture and color them, using the same colors.

Page 47
1 – teddy bear
3 – goats
6 – robots
8 – birds
10 – bees

Page 49
2 flowers
5 balloons
7 triangles

Page 50
trees – 6
flowers – 10
stones – 7
sun – 1

Page 53
4 kites
9 apples
5 cats
1 sun
10 birds
3 umbrellas
6 stones
8 bees
2 trees
7 flowers

Great Clarendon Street, Oxford, OX2 6DP, United Kingdom

Oxford University Press is a department of the University of Oxford.
It furthers the University's objective of excellence in research, scholarship,
and education by publishing worldwide. Oxford is a registered trade
mark of Oxford University Press in the UK and in certain other countries

ISBN: 978 0 19 486268 4   Little Blue Dot 1 Numeracy Book

Printed in China

This book is printed on paper from certified and well-managed sources

ACKNOWLEDGEMENTS

Illustrations by: Judy Brown. Spark character by Kevin Payne/Advocate
Art. Head outline p.12 by Mark Ruffle. *The publisher would like to thank the
following for permission to reproduce cover photographs:* Shutterstock (artjazz,
Avesun, _cz, Kitsana1980, piyaphon, Vandathai).